LEADERSHIP IN ACTION

50 HACKS TO UNLOCK POTENTIAL, RESOLVE CONFLICTS AND DRIVE CHANGE TO BECOME AN INCLUSIVE LEADER

MICHAEL L SEALY

First published by Mike Sealy 2024
Revised edition

Copyright © 2024 by Michael L Sealy

All rights reserved. No part of this publication may be reproduced, stored or transmitted in any form or by any means, electronic,

mechanical, photocopying, recording, scanning, or otherwise without

written permission from the publisher. It is illegal to copy this book, post it to a website, or distribute it by any other means without permission.

Michael L Sealy asserts the moral right to be identified as the author of this work.

Michael L Sealy has no responsibility for the persistence or accuracy of URLs for external or third-party Internet Websites referred to in this publication and does not guarantee that any content on such Websites is, or will remain, accurate or appropriate.

Designations used by companies to distinguish their products are often claimed as trademarks. All brand names and product names used in this book and on its cover are trade names, service marks, trademarks and registered trademarks of their respective owners. The publishers and the book are not associated with any product or vendor mentioned in this book. None of the companies referenced within the book have endorsed the book.

To my Mum,

Peggy Anita Sealy

You were the one who taught me love, resilience, and kindness. Though you are no longer with us, your presence continues to guide me in everything I do.

I miss you every day, love you deeply, and hope that I continue to make you proud in my actions and achievements.

This book is for you with all my heart.

TABLE OF CONTENTS

Foreword	7
Preface	9
Acknowledgments	15
Introduction	19
1. PERSONAL DEVELOPMENT FOR LEADERS	23
1. Cultivate Self-Awareness	23
2. Embrace a Growth Mindset	24
3. Develop Emotional Intelligence (EQ)	24
4. Develop Cultural Intelligence (CQ)	25
5. Prioritize Health and Well-Being	26
6. Set Clear Goals	27
7. Practice Humility	27
8. Foster Gratitude	28
9. Maintain Integrity	29
2. BUILDING STRONG RELATIONSHIP	31
10. Communicate Effectively	31
11. Empower Others	32
12. Foster Trust	32
13. Show Empathy	33
14. Build a Support Network	34
15. Celebrate Diversity	35
16. Give Constructive Feedback	35
17. Resolve Conflicts Effectively	36
18. Recognise and Reward Achievements	37
19. Be Approachable	37
3. LEADING TEAMS WITH IMPACT	39
20. Set a Clear Vision	39
21. Lead by Example	39

22. Encourage Collaboration	40
23. Promote Accountability	41
24. Develop Your Team	42
25. Manage Time Effectively	43
26. Make Decisions with Confidence	43
27. Stay Adaptable	44
28. Create Psychological Safety	45
29. Encourage Innovation	46
4. NAVIGATING CHALLENGES	47
30. Manage Stress Effectively	47
31. Deal with Failure Gracefully	48
32. Stay Calm Under Pressure	48
33. Tackle Difficult Conversations	49
34. Anticipate and Mitigate Risks	50
35. Lead Through Change	51
36. Manage Conflicting Priorities	51
37. Overcome Procrastination	52
38. Balance Short-Term and Long-Term Goals	53
39. Foster a Culture of Accountability	53
5. LEAVING A LEGACY	55
40. Mentor Future Leaders	55
41. Build a Strong Organisational Culture	56
42. Advocate for Ethical Practices	56
43. Make a Positive Impact	57
44. Practice Servant Leadership	57
45. Embrace Sustainability	58
46. Create Systems for Continuity	59
47. Share Your Vision	60
48. Write Your Leadership Philosophy	60
49. Reflect on Your Legacy	61
50. Champion Lifelong Learning	62
Conclusion	63
Resources	67

> Leadership is hard to define, and good leadership even harder. But if you can get people to follow you to the ends of the earth, you are a great leader.
>
> INDRA NOOYI (FORMER CEO, PEPSICO)

PREFACE

Why Do You Want to Become a Manager and Leader?

I assume that by buying this book, you aspire to become a manager or want to improve as a leader.

When coaching and mentoring colleagues aspiring to move into management, one of my key questions has always been: *Why do you want to become a manager?* The answers I've received over the years have been as varied as the individuals themselves, and often, they reflect surfacelevel motivations. Many see management as a natural sign of career progression, the next logical step, or promotion in their professional journey. Others are candid enough to admit that they view it as a way to increase their salary or gain more authority and status within the organisation. However, what I've rarely heard if ever, is someone expressing a genuine passion for people or a desire to foster and develop a high-performing team. Equally uncommon are answers that focus on driving business outcomes, improving processes, or aligning team efforts with organisational goals.

Expanding the Conversation

The answers to this question often reveal much about an individual's understanding of management and its challenges. Being a manager seems glamorous for many: more pay, power, and significant influence. However, the reality of management is far more complex. It's not just about overseeing tasks or earning a higher salary; it's about serving others, leading with empathy, navigating conflict, and taking accountability for the success or failure of your team.

Here are some common answers I've received and the responses I offer to encourage reflection and growth:

1. **"It's the next logical step in my career."**

Response: Advancing your career is important, but management isn't just about moving up a ladder; it's about shifting from individual to team success. Are you prepared to measure your accomplishments by the growth and achievements of others?

Being a manager means prioritising your team's needs over your own and finding satisfaction in their progress rather than just your milestones.

2. **"I want to earn more money."**

Response: It's honest and valid to want financial growth, but management brings responsibilities far beyond the higher salary. You'll need to handle difficult conversations, resolve conflicts, and make decisions that may not always be popular.

Are you ready to embrace the challenges and sacrifices that come with the added compensation? If financial growth is your primary goal, have you explored other career paths that don't involve managing people?

3. **"I want more authority and influence."**

Response: Authority in management is less about giving orders and more about earning trust and respect. Influence doesn't come from a title but from building relationships, demonstrating competence, and inspiring others.

Are you ready to lead by example, make the best decisions for your team, and take responsibility when things don't go as planned?

4. **"I want to make decisions and drive change."**

Response: Management does give you a platform to make decisions, but it's not always straightforward. You must balance your team's needs with the organisation's expectations.

Are you ready to take ownership of difficult decisions, communicate them effectively, and deal with the consequences if things don't go as planned? Change isn't just about implementing new ideas; it's about bringing people along with you.

5. "I want to help people grow and succeed."

Response: This is a strong motivation and a great starting point for leadership. However, mentoring and developing people takes time, patience, and a willingness to put their needs ahead of yours.

Are you prepared to invest in their success, even when it requires tough conversations or sacrifices on your part? Are you ready to celebrate their wins as if they were your own?

6. "I want to improve business outcomes and drive results."

Response: This is a practical and business-focused answer, but success as a manager depends on your ability to lead people to achieve those outcomes.

Are you ready to inspire, motivate, and guide a team toward shared goals? Management isn't just about setting targets; it's about enabling others to deliver on them.

Shifting the Perspective

When aspiring managers realise that management is about people and accountability, not just titles and perks, their perspectives often shift. This conversation is an opportunity to prepare them for the realities of leadership. It's not discouraging them but aligning their expectations with the role's demands. The most effective managers are those who step into the role with clarity, purpose, and a genuine desire to serve their team and organisation.

If someone's answers reflect a lack of understanding about management's responsibilities, it doesn't mean they can't succeed. Instead, it highlights areas where mentorship and development are needed. By encouraging honest self-reflection and offering constructive feedback,

we can help them approach leadership with the right mindset, making them not just managers but leaders who inspire, empower, and create meaningful impact.

ACKNOWLEDGMENTS

A Message of Deep Gratitude

I have enjoyed a fulfilling career as a manager and leader across multiple industries. This journey has been filled with incredible highs and inevitable lows, moments of anger, frustration, and even boredom. Yet, these challenges were always temporary, overshadowed by the enduring satisfaction of building high-performing teams and receiving the unwavering support and trust of my teams, peers, and leaders.

When I reflect on my career, what stands out most are the relationships that have shaped me, not just as a leader but as a person. The memories of outstanding colleagues, transformative experiences, and invaluable mentors remain my happy place. I owe so much of my growth to those who believed in me, coached and mentored me, sponsored my development, and invested in my potential through opportunities like business school and executive training programs.

This book is an acknowledgement with deep gratitude to everyone who has played a role in my career and believed in my ability to lead. Your trust, support, and influence have profoundly impacted me, and I hope this book reflects the values and lessons I've gained from you. While I wish I could acknowledge every single person, there are a few who must be mentioned for their extraordinary contributions to my journey:

- **The Rules of the Garage Mentoring Circle:** For 25 years, this group has been a constant source of wisdom, camaraderie, and inspiration. Thank you to **Peter Gaarn, Deb Colden, Betty Sproule, Isabella Phoenix, Subbu Vempati,** and **Jaime Reyes**(RIP). Our quarterly meetings remain a cherished cornerstone of my personal and professional life.
- **Bernard Meric:** As the former Managing Director and Senior Vice President of EMEA at Hewlett-Packard, Bernard mentored me for 12 transformative months. His guidance on business strategies while he headed HP's wide-format printing division in Barcelona opened my eyes to the intricacies of leadership at scale.
- **Molly Stehr:** The best leader I ever had the privilege of reporting to at Microsoft. Molly's passion, support, trust, and advocacy set a gold standard for leadership. I often tell people how I told her I'd run through brick walls for her, and I meant it. Her belief in me changed my life.
- **Denise Rundle:** As GM of Microsoft Services and Support, Denise was a beacon of wisdom and encouragement. Her ability to make time for me, particularly during my visits to Seattle, left an indelible mark on my perspective and confidence as a leader.

- **Gary Nugent:** My first boss at Informa, Gary epitomised inclusive leadership. His trust and commitment allowed me the autonomy to shape and develop the client services team with the knowledge and experiences I accumulated. His leadership inspired me to lead with trust and collaboration.
- **Lord Stephen A. Carter CBE:** Group CEO at Informa and my partner in the reverse mentoring program. Getting to know him personally was an honour, and I am forever grateful for the opportunity to learn from him. I'm not sure he fully realises his impact on me, but our mentoring relationship will remain one of the most treasured memories of my career.

To everyone mentioned here and to the many others who believed in me and supported me, thank you from the bottom of my heart. Your trust, encouragement, and influence have shaped the leader I am today. This book is as much a testament to your impact as it reflects my journey. You have changed my life, and I will always be deeply grateful.

INTRODUCTION

As a manager and leader in corporate environments, I've navigated a landscape filled with successes and setbacks. Each step of my journey has left its mark, shaping not only the professional I am today but also the person I strive to be every day. I've celebrated victories that reinforced my belief in the power of teamwork and innovation, but I've also faced challenging moments that tested my resilience, character and emotions. I've made my fair share of mistakes, some small and forgettable, others significant enough to result in reprimands that impacted my performance review rating and yearend rewards. Yet, these experiences, no matter how difficult, were never wasted. They became powerful lessons that pushed me to grow, adapt, and refine my leadership approach.

I've learned that leadership is not a static destination but an evolving journey. Early in my career, I believed, through observation, that leadership was about authority and control, ensuring tasks were completed and objectives met. But as the years passed, I realised it was far more complex and meaningful. Authentic leadership is about influence, inspiration, and impact. It's about understanding the people you work with, valuing their perspectives, and creating an environment where they feel empowered to thrive.

One of the most profound aspects of my journey has been the opportunity to work under a broad spectrum of leaders, some exceptional, others less so. I've had the privilege of learning from managers who led with empathy, clarity, and vision. They showed me how to foster trust, build high-performing teams, and gracefully navigate change. But I've also experienced the challenges of working with leaders who lacked these qualities, those who micromanaged, failed to communicate effectively, or made decisions that stifled growth and morale. While these experiences were challenging at the time, they offered invaluable lessons. They taught me what not to do and inspired me to strive to be a leader who uplifts rather than diminishes.

Becoming an inclusive leader has been one of the most transformative aspects of my leadership journey. It's a continuous process of growth and learning, a commitment to embracing diversity, seeking out different perspectives, and creating spaces where everyone feels valued and heard. I've come to understand that inclusivity isn't just a "nice to-have" quality in leadership; it's a necessity for fostering innovation, collaboration, and trust. It requires self-awareness, humility, and a willingness to acknowledge and address blind spots.

Through all the triumphs and trials, one truth has remained constant: leadership is a skill that defines the success of individuals, teams, and organisations. It's not about being perfect; it's about showing up, learning from your mistakes, and striving to improve daily. Each experience, whether uplifting or challenging, has contributed to the leader I am today and the leader I aspire to become tomorrow.

Reflecting on my journey, I'm reminded that leadership is not just a professional responsibility but a personal calling. It's about positively impacting the people you lead and the environments you influence. I embrace that responsibility with humility, gratitude, and a steadfast commitment to growth.

This book presents 50 practical and actionable leadership hacks that can be applied universally, no matter the size or nature of the team or organisation you lead. These strategies are designed to empower you, boost your effectiveness, and foster an environment where growth and success thrive. To bring these concepts to life, I'll share real-world examples from my own experiences and observations of others in leadership roles.

It's important to acknowledge that leadership is never a one-size-fits all approach. Every decision and action a leader takes is influenced by their unique circumstances and shaped by their personal experiences, upbringing, education, and values. No template can account for the complexity of these variables. Instead, this book serves as a guide and, hopefully, a source of inspiration, a resource to help you reflect, learn, and grow. Whether you're looking to fine-tune your leadership style or completely transform certain behaviours, I hope this book will support your ongoing journey toward becoming your best leader.

The book is designed to be more than a guide; it's a workbook and a companion. Use the exercises to implement these hacks and reflect on the anecdotes as inspiration for your journey. Your leadership style is unique and shaped by your experiences and insights. Revisit these pages often, adding your own stories and growth milestones.

CHAPTER 1
PERSONAL DEVELOPMENT FOR LEADERS

1. CULTIVATE SELF-AWARENESS

The ability to consciously recognise and understand your emotions, thoughts, behaviours, and their impact on others. It involves being attuned to your internal world (values, beliefs, motivations, and biases) and your external interactions (how others perceive and respond to you).

Hack: Understand your strengths, weaknesses, and values through regular self-reflection. Use tools like personality assessments or journaling.

Exercise: Write down three situations where you succeeded and three where you struggled. Analyse the common traits of both scenarios.

Anecdote: As a leader of a team of field service engineers, I would periodically go out to customer sites with the engineers to observe performance. When an engineer was stuck or had difficulty resolving the issue, I would often jump in and take over. I realised I was micromanaging these time-pressure situations, which stifled team development. By stepping back and trusting my team, outcomes improved.

Your Example: Reflect on when self-awareness helped or hindered a leadership outcome. What did you learn?

2. EMBRACE A GROWTH MINDSET

The belief is that abilities, intelligence, and talents can be developed through dedication, effort, and learning. It contrasts with a fixed mindset, where individuals believe these traits are innate and unchangeable.

Hack: Treat challenges as opportunities to learn. Reframe failure as feedback.

Exercise: Write down a recent failure. Identify three lessons learned and how you'll apply them.

Anecdote: Thomas Edison famously said, "I have not failed. I've just found 10,000 ways that won't work." This mindset kept him innovating.

Your Example: Describe a time when you persisted through a challenge. What did you learn?

3. DEVELOP EMOTIONAL INTELLIGENCE (EQ)

The ability to recognise, understand, manage, and influence emotions, both your own and those of others. It is critical in personal and professional relationships, enabling individuals to navigate social complexities, communicate effectively, and make informed decisions.

Hack: Improve your ability to understand and manage emotions: practice self-regulation, empathy, and active listening.

Exercise: Keep a daily emotion journal. Note your emotional triggers and how you responded.

Anecdote: An HR manager shared how empathetic listening during a conflict resolved a misunderstanding that could have led to turnover.

Your Example: Think of a time when showing empathy helped resolve an issue.

4. DEVELOP CULTURAL INTELLIGENCE (CQ)

Recognising, understanding, and adapting to cultural differences in values, communication styles, and behaviours. It is essential to foster collaboration in diverse environments and effectively navigate global or multicultural settings.

Hack: Enhance your ability to work across cultures by practising cultural awareness, adaptability, and openness. Take time to learn about cultural norms and values, seek diverse perspectives, and approach differences with curiosity rather than judgment.

Exercise: Engage in a "cultural curiosity challenge." Each week, learn about one aspect of a culture unfamiliar to you, such as a tradition, value system, or communication style, and reflect on how it differs from or aligns with your experiences.

Anecdote: On my many travels to visit colleagues or suppliers in different parts of the world, I have always made a point of learning a few basic phrases in the native language; I found that this broke the ice and created a sense of trust and respect, leading to smoother collaborations and stronger relationships.

Your Example: Recall a time when you tried to understand someone's cultural perspective. How did it impact your interaction or the outcome of the situation?

5. PRIORITIZE HEALTH AND WELL-BEING

A state of physical, mental, and social well-being in which an individual is free from illness or injury and can function effectively in daily life. It encompasses not only the absence of disease but also favourable conditions supporting vitality and longevity.

Hack: Ensure you are mentally and physically fit. Leadership requires stamina.

Exercise: Create a weekly schedule including at least three 30-minute physical activities and one mindfulness exercise.

Anecdote: I committed to putting my health and well-being before a job or work through several activities or behavioural changes, like going to the gym 4-5 times a week and ensuring that I take regular breaks throughout the day.

Note: Attending back-to-back meetings all day is not productive and creates a barrier for your team to engage with you.

Your Example: Describe how your health habits impact your leadership performance. Are you taking breaks, eating nutritional food, or exercising?

6. SET CLEAR GOALS

Defining specific, measurable, and achievable objectives that provide direction and focus. Clear goals outline what you want to achieve, why it is essential, and how success will be measured.

Hack: Clear, measurable goals provide direction and inspire confidence. Great leaders align their personal and professional objectives

with their organisation's vision.

Anecdote: I have always found working without clearly defined goals challenging. When managing teams, I like to set clear goals that cascade down to individual goals with a regular cadence of tracking and measuring.

Exercise: Write down one personal and one professional goal using the SMART (**S**pecific, **M**easurable, **A**chievable, **R**elevant, **T**ime-Bound) framework.

7. PRACTICE HUMILITY

Being modest, respectful, and unassuming is marked by a clear understanding of one's strengths and limitations and a genuine willingness to learn from others. It entails acknowledging that success is rarely achieved alone and appreciating the contributions of others without arrogance or self-centredness.

Hack: Humility allows you to recognise the contributions of others and admit when you're wrong. It shifts the focus from being the best to bringing out the best in others.

Anecdote: After a high-profile project failure, my project manager immediately notified me and took full accountability. I acknowledged her oversight, and together, we sought input from her team on how to improve. His humility rebuilt trust and encouraged team members to share ideas and concerns, strengthening collaboration openly.

Exercise:

1. Reflect on a time when you were wrong but hesitated to admit it. Write down how the situation unfolded and how taking responsibility might have changed the outcome.
2. Choose one day this week to praise others' contributions. Start every meeting with at least one acknowledgement of a team member's success.
3. Practice saying "I don't know" when faced with questions outside your expertise. Follow up with a plan to find answers.

8. FOSTER GRATITUDE

The quality of being thankful and showing appreciation for the kindness, benefits, or gifts received, whether from others, circumstances, or life itself. It is an acknowledgement and recognition of the positive aspects of one's life, regardless of challenges or hardships.

Hack: Gratitude enhances workplace morale by recognising the value of others' efforts. Leaders who regularly express appreciation foster loyalty and a positive work culture.

Anecdote: I have always prioritised recognising exceptional performance and the "above and beyond" efforts of my team, whether through a personal thank you or public acknowledgement. As a leader, your success is intrinsically tied to your team; they are the driving force behind every achievement. Never forget that their contributions are what make the difference between success and failure.

Exercise:

1. Send personalised thank you notes to three team members, highlighting specific contributions.
2. Create a "kudos board" in your workspace where team members can publicly recognise each other's achievements.

9. MAINTAIN INTEGRITY

Being honest, ethical, and consistent in one's actions, values, principles, and intentions. It means adhering to moral and ethical standards, even when inconvenient, unpopular, or complex. A person with integrity aligns with their beliefs and values, ensuring that their behaviour reflects their words and promises.

Hack: Integrity is the cornerstone of trust. Consistently acting honestly and aligning your actions with your values earns respect and credibility from your team.

Anecdote: Leaders must do what is right, not just what is easy, because authentic leadership is about integrity and long-term impact. Choosing the right path, even when challenging, builds trust, inspires respect, and sets a standard for others to follow. Easy decisions may provide temporary relief, but doing what is right ensures sustainable success and reinforces the values that define exceptional leadership.

Exercise: Write down your top three core values and how they guide your leadership decisions.

CHAPTER 2
BUILDING STRONG RELATIONSHIP

10. COMMUNICATE EFFECTIVELY

To convey information, thoughts, or feelings clearly and in a way that is easily understood by others. It involves not only the ability to articulate your message but also to listen actively, adapt your communication style to your audience, and ensure mutual understanding.

Hack: Clear communication is the foundation of any successful relationship. Influential leaders actively listen, adapt their communication styles, and ensure their messages are understood and actionable.

Exercise: Role-play difficult conversations with a trusted peer and practice active listening.

***Anecdote*:** A Dutch employee who reported to me did not realise that his directive tone alienated his colleagues. He shifted to a more collaborative style and improved team morale.

Your Example: Recall a time when communication broke down. How did you address it?

11. EMPOWER OTHERS

The process of giving people the tools, resources, authority, and confidence they need to take ownership of their responsibilities, make decisions, and achieve their potential. It involves creating an environment where individuals feel trusted and valued and can contribute meaningfully to a shared goal.

Hack: Delegate tasks and trust your team to handle them. Provide clear instructions and support.

Exercise: List three tasks you can delegate this week. Choose someone for each and set clear expectations.

Anecdote: An overwhelmed HR Director insisted on maintaining control over every aspect of the business, which often caused delays and bottlenecks, creating a feeling of mistrust and frustration with some of his leaders.

Your Example: Reflect on when delegation went well or poorly. What could you improve?

12. FOSTER TRUST

The confidence or belief in the reliability, integrity, honesty, and ability of someone or something. It is a foundational element of relationships, enabling effective collaboration, communication, and mutual respect. Trust fosters a sense of safety and dependability, encouraging people to rely on one another without fear of betrayal or harm.

Hack: Trust is the foundation of leadership. Be transparent, keep your promises, and demonstrate reliability.

Exercise: Ask team members anonymously to rate their trust level in your leadership on a scale of 1–10 and provide feedback on how you can improve.

Anecdote: A department manager noticed low trust levels after employees hesitated to share feedback during meetings. After being transparent about company challenges and admitting his mistakes, the manager saw trust improve, with team members contributing ideas more freely.

Example: If you promise to send a follow-up email or resolve an issue, ensure you do so within the agreed timeframe. Repeatedly honouring commitments builds trust over time.

13. SHOW EMPATHY

The ability to understand, recognise, and share another person's feelings, thoughts, and perspectives. It involves identifying what someone else is experiencing emotionally or mentally and responding

with compassion and care. Empathy bridges the gap between people, fostering connection, trust, and effective communication.

Hack: Understand and acknowledge the feelings and perspectives of others. Empathy builds more robust connections and trust.

Exercise: During one-on-one meetings, ask open-ended questions like, "How are you feeling about your current workload?" or "Is there anything you'd like more support with?" Practice active listening by summarising what you've heard before responding.

Your Example: Create a habit of checking in with your team, not just about work but their well-being. A simple "How are you doing?" can make a big difference.

14. BUILD A SUPPORT NETWORK

A group of individuals or resources that provide guidance, encouragement, advice, and assistance during times of need or in pursuit of goals. This network includes mentors, peers, friends, family, colleagues, professional advisors, organisations, and communities. A strong support network helps individuals navigate challenges, make better decisions, and sustain emotional and mental well-being.

Hack: Surround yourself with mentors, peers, and advisors who can provide guidance and feedback. Leadership can be lonely, especially during crises or when making difficult decisions. A support network helps you stay grounded and offers fresh ideas or solutions.

Exercise:

- Identify three people in your professional circle who inspire you. Contact them for coffee or a virtual chat to seek advice or build a stronger connection.
- Join a leadership or industry-specific group to expand your network.

Your Example: Schedule quarterly "mentor sessions" with someone whose leadership you admire. Share your challenges and goals and invite feedback.

15. CELEBRATE DIVERSITY

Diversity refers to the presence and inclusion of a wide range of individual differences and perspectives within a group, organisation, or society. These differences can include, but are not limited to, race, ethnicity, gender, age, sexual orientation, socio-economic background, physical abilities, neurodiversity, religious beliefs, and cultural backgrounds. Diversity also encompasses differences in experiences, viewpoints, and ways of thinking.

Hack: Embrace diverse perspectives and backgrounds. Inclusive leadership drives innovation and collaboration.

Exercise: Conduct a team diversity inventory by listing each member's unique skills, experiences, and perspectives.

Example: Establish a policy where all team members contribute ideas during meetings, ensuring quieter individuals have the chance to speak.

Use anonymous idea submission tools if necessary.

16. GIVE CONSTRUCTIVE FEEDBACK

A form of communication aimed at helping someone improve their performance, behaviour, or outcomes by providing specific, actionable, and supportive insights. Unlike criticism, which can focus solely on what is wrong, constructive feedback highlights areas for improvement and ways to achieve success, fostering growth and learning.

Hack: Deliver specific, actionable feedback and focus on improvement.

Exercise: When sharing feedback with an employee, Ask for their perspective.

Anecdote: A team leader kept providing vague feedback to their direct report about his performance, confusing the employee. After switching to specific, constructive feedback, the employee understood how to improve and was able to improve his performance.

Your Example: Instead of saying, "Your reports need improvement," which is vague, try, "In last week's report, I noticed some data inaccu-

racies that could confuse stakeholders. Double checking your sources will improve clarity and trust."

17. RESOLVE CONFLICTS EFFECTIVELY

Conflicts refer to disagreements, disputes, or clashes between individuals, groups, or entities arising from differing opinions, values, interests, goals, or needs. Conflicts are a natural part of human interaction and can occur in personal, professional, or social settings.

Hack: Address conflicts head-on with a focus on collaboration and finding mutually beneficial solutions.

Exercise: Avoid team conflicts by facilitating brainstorming sessions to explore win-win solutions.

Example: Create a conflict resolution process where employees can escalate issues to you early, ensuring they feel heard before tensions escalate.

18. RECOGNISE AND REWARD ACHIEVEMENTS

The successful completion or attainment of a goal, task, or objective through effort, skill, or perseverance. It is often marked by a sense of satisfaction, recognition, or progress and can be individual or collective in nature.

Hack: Celebrate milestones and individual contributions to keep your team motivated.

Exercise: Celebrate achievements by using a rotating "Team Spotlight" in meetings.

Anecdote: In my monthly team meetings, I would ask managers to identify their top performers of the month. We would collectively review the candidates to select an overall top performer who would receive an Amazon gift voucher. I would also follow up with a personal email to all the top performers in recognition of their hard work and commitment to the team.

Your Example: Write handwritten notes of appreciation for standout performances. A personal touch can leave a lasting impression.

19. BE APPROACHABLE

The quality of being friendly, open, and accessible to interact with, making others feel comfortable initiating conversations, sharing ideas, or seeking guidance. An approachable person fosters trust, encourages communication, and creates an inviting atmosphere that puts others at ease.

Hack: Encourage open communication by being approachable and receptive to feedback.

Exercise: Keep your office door open (literally or metaphorically) for at least one hour each day, encouraging team members to drop by with questions or concerns.

Anecdote: I worked for a manager who kept his office door closed when he was in the office; I quickly learned not to rely on him for support.

Example: Set up regular one-on-one check-ins with your team, focusing on their needs and concerns. Reassure them that no issue is too small to discuss.

CHAPTER 3
LEADING TEAMS WITH IMPACT

20. SET A CLEAR VISION

A well-defined and compelling picture of the desired future or goal and a roadmap. It provides purpose, direction, and focus, aligning individuals or teams around shared objectives and inspiring action.

Hack: Inspire your team with a well-defined vision. Tie it to shared values and goals.

Exercise: Write down your team's current goals. Align them with your long-term vision and share it in your next meeting.

Your Example: What is your vision for your team or organisation? Please write it down.

21. LEAD BY EXAMPLE

Demonstrate the behaviours, attitudes, and values you expect from others through your actions. It involves embodying the principles you want your team or peers to follow and setting a standard for others to emulate. By modelling desired behaviour, leaders inspire trust, respect, and alignment within their teams.

Hack: Demonstrate the behaviours and attitudes you expect from your team.

Exercise: Reflect on three core values or behaviours you expect from your team (e.g., punctuality, commitment, adaptability). Observe your interactions and decisions for one week, noting gaps between your expectations and conduct. Adjust as necessary.

Anecdote: Before asking my team to complete mandatory compliance training, I ensure I complete it beforehand.

Your Example: If you expect your team to be punctual, consistently arrive early to meetings. If collaboration is a priority, actively participate in brainstorming sessions instead of delegating the task to others.

22. ENCOURAGE COLLABORATION

The process of individuals or groups working together toward a common goal or purpose by leveraging their collective skills, knowledge, and resources. It emphasises teamwork, mutual respect, and open communication to achieve outcomes that are often more effective than

what any individual could accomplish alone.

Hack: Create an environment where team members feel encouraged to share ideas and work together.

***Exercise*:** Pair team members with complementary skills on a small project to encourage cross-functional collaboration.

***Your Example*:** Set up a shared online platform (like SharePoint) where team members can contribute ideas, comment on others' suggestions, and track project progress.

23. PROMOTE ACCOUNTABILITY

The obligation and willingness to take responsibility for one's actions, decisions, and outcomes, whether positive or negative. It involves being answerable to oneself, others, or a group for fulfilling commitments and achieving agreed-upon goals.

Hack: Set clear expectations and hold yourself and your team accountable for results.

Exercise: Conduct weekly check-ins where team members report progress and discuss obstacles.

Anecdote: In regular 1:1s with my team, I asked them to complete a monthly AIP form (Achievements, Issues, Priorities). The process created a culture of accountability without blame, helping to improve individual performance.

Your Example: If a team member misses a deadline, address it promptly in a one-on-one meeting. Focus on understanding the reasons and collaborating on solutions to prevent recurrence.

24. DEVELOP YOUR TEAM

The intentional process of enhancing the skills, knowledge, capabilities, and confidence of team members to enable them to excel in their roles and grow professionally. It involves providing opportunities for learning, fostering a supportive environment, and empowering individuals to reach their full potential.

Hack: Invest in the growth and development of your team members by providing training and opportunities for advancement.

Exercise: Create a development plan with measurable milestones for each team member, such as completing a course, taking on a challenging project, or attending a conference.

Anecdote: I once had a high-potential employee who showed great interest in analytics. By assigning him data-driven tasks for the team, funding software tools, and taking a training course, he advanced into a specialised role, boosting morale, team loyalty, and greater productivity for the team.

Your Example: Dedicate a portion of the team budget for professional development, such as workshops, certifications, or coaching programs.

Celebrate milestones achieved as a result of this investment.

25. MANAGE TIME EFFECTIVELY

Organising, planning, and allocating your time effectively to accomplish tasks and achieve goals in a structured and efficient manner. It involves prioritising activities, minimising distractions, and making deliberate choices about how to use time to maximise productivity and reduce stress.

Hack: As a leader, optimise your productivity by prioritising tasks and avoiding unnecessary meetings. Ensure sufficient time for your employees to engage and connect with you beyond the formal one-on-one process.

Exercise: Regularly audit your meeting schedule for one month and identify which meetings could be shortened, combined, or eliminated.

Example of Action: Implement and respect a "no meeting day" policy once a week, giving your team uninterrupted time to focus on their

work.

26. MAKE DECISIONS WITH CONFIDENCE

The ability to evaluate options, choose a course of action, and commit to it with clarity and self-assurance. It involves trusting your judgment, relying on available information, and accepting accountability for the outcomes, even in the face of uncertainty or complexity.

Hack: Gather input, analyse information, and make timely decisions that align with your goals.

***Exercise*:** Before making an important decision, list three potential options and their pros and cons. Use a decision-making framework like SWOT (Strengths, Weaknesses, Opportunities, Threats) analysis to evaluate each option. Seek input from critical stakeholders but set a firm deadline for finalising your choice.

***Example of Action*:** Create a simple decision-making flowchart with input from relevant team members for significant decisions. Use this tool to communicate the rationale behind your choice, ensuring transparency and confidence.

27. STAY ADAPTABLE

Maintain flexibility and openness to change in new circumstances, challenges, or opportunities. It involves adjusting plans, behaviours, or strategies quickly and effectively while focusing on overarching goals. Adaptable individuals and leaders thrive in dynamic environments by embracing uncertainty and finding creative solutions.

Hack: Flexibility in leadership allows you to thrive in changing circumstances.

Exercise: Identify one significant change you've faced in the past year.

List three ways you adapted or could have adapted better.

Your Example: Describe a situation where adaptability was crucial to your success.

28. CREATE PSYCHOLOGICAL SAFETY

A shared belief within a team or group that it is safe to take risks, express opinions, ask questions and admit mistakes without fear of embarrassment, criticism, or retribution. It is a foundational

element of trust that encourages open communication, creativity, and collaboration.

Hack: Ensure team members feel safe expressing themselves without fear of criticism or retribution.

Exercise: Conduct a confidential survey asking team members to rate how safe they feel sharing opinions or admitting mistakes. Use the feedback to identify areas for improvement.

Anecdote: At a tech company I worked at, one of the engineers constantly hesitated to get out on site to complete his service calls,

which caused a delay and did not impact his teams, who would have to take the service calls that would not otherwise be completed on that day. After discussing his concerns and learning that he was afraid to fail in front of the customer, he was encouraged to get out there and call for help if ever he was stuck. This approach encouraged him to admit and address issues promptly, ultimately preventing more significant problems further down the line and increasing his confidence.

Your Example: Share your mistakes and what you learned from them to normalise imperfection and growth.

Create a team charter emphasising respect, listening, and non judgmental feedback in all discussions.

29. ENCOURAGE INNOVATION

Creating, improving, or implementing new ideas, methods, products, or services that add value or solve problems. It involves thinking creatively, challenging the status quo, and applying fresh approaches to meet existing or emerging needs.

Hack: Support creativity and risk-taking to drive growth and problem-solving. As a leader, demonstrate and be transparent about your confidence to take risks and sometimes fail.

Exercise: Host a "blue-sky thinking" session where team members brainstorm unconventional ideas without worrying about feasibility.

Create a no-judgment zone to encourage free thinking.

Anecdote: At 3M, an employee named Art Fry used the company's

15% "innovation time" to experiment with adhesive properties. His idea eventually led to creating Post-it Notes, one of 3M's most iconic products. The company's culture of innovation and risk-taking made this possible.

Your Example: Foster a "Fail Fast" Mindset: Encourage team members to take calculated risks and view failure as an opportunity to learn.

CHAPTER 4
NAVIGATING CHALLENGES

30. MANAGE STRESS EFFECTIVELY

It is recognising, reducing, and coping with the physical, emotional, and psychological demands caused by challenging or overwhelming situations. Effective stress management involves using techniques and strategies to maintain balance, build resilience, and improve overall

well-being while navigating life's pressures.

Hack: Be mindful of your team's workload and working hours and ensure they are allowed to take breaks and have fun

Exercise: Develop techniques to handle stress, such as mindfulness, delegation, and prioritisation.

Your Example: How do you handle stress during high-pressure situations? What works best for you?

31. DEAL WITH FAILURE GRACEFULLY

The inability to achieve a desired goal, outcome, or expectation. It occurs when efforts, plans, or actions do not produce the intended results, leading to setbacks, disappointment, or missed opportunities. While failure is often viewed negatively, it is a natural and valuable part of growth and learning.

Hack: Accept responsibility for failures, learn from them, and move forward positively. Failure is not the end; it's an opportunity to grow, learn and refine your approach.

Exercise: Reflect on a recent failure or setback you've experienced.

- What went wrong, and why?
- What did you learn about yourself or the process?
- What could you do differently next time?

32. STAY CALM UNDER PRESSURE

The feeling of stress, urgency, or intense demand placed on an individual due to external or internal factors. It arises when there is a perceived need to meet high expectations, deadlines, responsibilities, or challenges, often with limited time or resources. Pressure can be motivating in some cases but overwhelming if not managed effectively.

Hack: Maintain composure in high-stakes situations to instil confidence in your team. Leaders who stay calm provide stability and clarity during uncertainty.

Exercise: Focus on what's most urgent and essential to reduce overwhelm.

Your Example:

1. Recall a high-pressure situation where you struggled to stay calm. Reflect on how your emotions affected your decision-making and your team.
2. Practice a calming technique, such as box breathing:

- Inhale for 4 seconds.
- Hold your breath for 4 seconds.
- Exhale for 4 seconds.
- Hold again for 4 seconds. Repeat for 1–2 minutes.

33. TACKLE DIFFICULT CONVERSATIONS

Discussions involving sensitive, emotionally charged, or challenging topics. They often trigger strong emotions and may include conflicts or uncomfortable truths. Handling them carefully is essential for clear communication, respect, and constructive outcomes. Examples include performance feedback, personal grievances, or addressing sensitive issues.

Hack: Approach challenging discussions with empathy and focus on solutions.

Exercise: Write a script for your following challenging conversation, including critical points and empathetic statements.

Anecdote: I resolved the tension created by a high-performing but disruptive employee disrupting the rest of the team with selfish behaviour by opening an honest dialogue about expectations and support. Initially, he continued to be argumentative, and I politely explained that he also had a choice if he felt he was too good to be part of my team. He later thought about the conversation and apologised to me and a public apology to the team. It was a difficult discussion, but leaders must have the courage to tackle it head-on and not think the situation will blow over in time.

Your Example: Consider a tough conversation you've had or need to have. What would you do differently next time?

34. ANTICIPATE AND MITIGATE RISKS

Identifying, assessing, and taking steps to reduce or control potential risks. It involves creating strategies and actions to minimise the impact of risks, ensuring they are less severe or manageable if they occur.

Hack: Proactively identify potential risks before they occur and create contingency plans to address them.

Exercise*:* Create a risk assessment matrix where you identify potential risks, rate their probability and impact, and plan mitigation strategies.

Your Example*:* Regularly evaluate potential risks in your business and operations and create contingency plans to address them before they occur.

35. LEAD THROUGH CHANGE

The ability to guide a team through change and transformation by clearly communicating the purpose, process, and expected outcomes, helping them adapt and stay focused during these periods.

Hack: During change, empower "change champions" across your organisation to effectively communicate key messages, address concerns, and gather team feedback.

Exercise: Create a communication plan for upcoming changes, outlining who needs to know what, when, and how. Ensure the change's purpose, process, and expected outcomes are included.

Anecdote: When a large company undertook an acquisition, the CEO regularly updated employees and set up town halls to address concerns. By clearly outlining the reasons for the acquisition, the benefits, and the steps involved, employees felt more confident about the transition.

Your Example: Think of a time when you led a change or transition; what worked well and what didn't work so well, and what would you do differently next time?

36. MANAGE CONFLICTING PRIORITIES

Juggling multiple demands can lead to confusion and burnout. Leaders must focus on prioritisation to ensure teams work efficiently.

Hack*:* During times of change, communicate openly and frequently with your team about the why, how, and what to expect, ensuring everyone feels informed and included.

Exercise*:* Categorise your tasks into urgent vs Important. Focus on urgent and important tasks first, then delegate or schedule less urgent ones.

Your Example: When you previously had conflicting priorities, what tactics did you use to resolve the situation?

37. OVERCOME PROCRASTINATION

Delaying or postponing tasks or actions is often due to a lack of motivation, fear of failure, or feeling overwhelmed, despite knowing that completing them is important.

Hack: Break large, daunting tasks into smaller, more manageable steps and use techniques like the Pomodoro method to stay focused and avoid delays.

Exercise*:* Pomodoro Technique

- Break your work into 25-minute focused intervals (Pomodoros), followed by a 5-minute break. After four Pomodoros, take a more extended break.

Anecdote*:* Working for a leader who procrastinates over a decision quickly becomes the bottleneck that can miss deadlines or cause other problems

Your Example*:* Be prepared to decide to move forward even when you only have 70% of the needed information.

38. BALANCE SHORT-TERM AND LONG-TERM GOALS

Short-term goals are objectives expected to be achieved soon, typically within a few days, weeks, or months. They focus on immediate tasks or milestones. Long-term goals are objectives set for a distant future, usually months or years. They focus on broader, more significant achievements and outcomes.

Hack: Maintain a focus on immediate tasks while planning for long-term success.

Exercise: SMART Goals

- Set SMART (Specific, Measurable, Achievable, Relevant, Timebound) goals for both short-term and long-term objectives. Review your goals regularly to stay aligned with both immediate needs and plans.

Anecdote*:* I have seen leaders only focus on the short term and ignore the longer-term goal, which is short-sighted as it prevents working on the plans that lead to long-term success

39. FOSTER A CULTURE OF ACCOUNTABILITY

An environment where individuals take responsibility for their actions, decisions, and outcomes. It involves clear expectations, transparent communication, and regular feedback, fostering a sense of ownership and ensuring everyone is responsible for their roles and contributions.

***Hack*:** Encourage team members to take ownership of their responsibilities and hold themselves accountable for their actions.

Exercise*:* Accountability Partners

- Pair team members with accountability partners to regularly check in on progress. This encourages personal responsibility and allows for peer support.

Your Example: How have you managed the accountability of your team? During one-to-ones with your team members, address accountability for their tasks to ensure ownership and responsibility.

CHAPTER 5
LEAVING A LEGACY

40. MENTOR FUTURE LEADERS

Guiding, supporting, and inspiring individuals with the potential to grow into leadership roles.

Hack: Invest time in developing the next generation by providing guidance, sharing your experiences, and offering constructive feedback.

Exercise: Pair up with a younger or less experienced colleague and offer to meet for monthly mentoring sessions, focusing on skill-building leadership qualities and career development.

Anecdote: I have mentored many colleagues, helping them develop and grow their potential to become managers and leaders. I have also had several mentors who contributed to developing my leadership skills.

Your Example: Identify and support emerging leaders within your team to ensure a pipeline of future leadership.

41. BUILD A STRONG ORGANISATIONAL CULTURE

The shared values, beliefs, behaviours, and practices shape how people within an organisation interact with each other and approach their work. It encompasses the unwritten norms and expectations that influence decision-making, communication, and the work environment.

Hack*:* Define and model the core values you want to cultivate in your organisation and ensure they are reflected in daily behaviours and decisions.

Exercise*:* Hold a workshop with your team to discuss the organisation's values and how to embody them in your work. Then, work with your DEI lead to create a culture of inclusion and actively promote these values.

Your Example*:* How do your daily actions reflect the values you want to establish in your organisation's culture?

42. ADVOCATE FOR ETHICAL PRACTICES

Actions and decisions that align with accepted moral principles, ensuring fairness, integrity, transparency, and responsibility in business and personal conduct. These practices involve adhering to legal standards, respecting rights, and making choices that promote trust and accountability while considering the broader impact on society and the environment.

Hack: Ensure ethics are at the forefront of all decisions. Lead by example, upholding integrity and transparency in all actions.

Exercise: Review a current decision through an ethical lens, considering potential conflicts of interest, fairness, and long-term impact. Share your findings with your team and seek their input.

Your Example: What are you doing to strengthen your commitment to ethical decision-making in the face of competing pressures?

43. MAKE A POSITIVE IMPACT

The beneficial influence or effect of actions, decisions, or initiatives on individuals, communities, organisations, or society. It involves creating value, improving well-being, and contributing to long-term, sustainable growth while fostering positive environmental change, social equity, or economic development.

Hack: Focus on creating value through your leadership, whether within your organisation or community and ensure that your actions are aligned with this purpose.

Exercise: Identify one area within your organisation or community where you can make a positive difference and take actionable steps toward improving it.

Your Example: What is one impactful change you could implement in your organisation to create more excellent value for the business?

44. PRACTICE SERVANT LEADERSHIP

Leaders focus on serving others, empowering their team, and fostering a supportive, collaborative environment rather than seeking power or recognition for themselves. This approach emphasises humility, empathy, and a commitment to developing others.

Hack: Prioritize the needs of your team and organisation over your own. Empower others by providing support and resources to help them succeed.

Exercise: Hold a meeting where you actively listen to your team's concerns and suggestions, demonstrating that their needs are your priority. Act on their feedback.

Your Example: How can you better serve your team to ensure they feel supported and empowered?

45. EMBRACE SUSTAINABILITY

The practice of meeting present needs without compromising the ability of future generations to meet their own, focusing on responsible resource use and long-term environmental, social, and economic health.

Hack: Incorporate environmentally and socially responsible practices into your leadership by making sustainable decisions in your business operations and stakeholder interactions.

Exercise: Review your team's sustainability practices and identify areas for improvement, such as reducing waste or supporting local communities.

Anecdote: A company's CEO implemented sustainability initiatives that reduced environmental impact, saved money in the long term, and proved that sustainability can be both ethically and financially beneficial. As a result, they have become a globally recognised multi-award winning company.

Your Example: How can you incorporate more sustainable practices into your leadership approach and organisation's strategy?

46. CREATE SYSTEMS FOR CONTINUITY

Processes, structures, and strategies are implemented to ensure that an organisation can continue operating smoothly and effectively, even without critical leaders or during disruptions. These systems help maintain operations, preserve knowledge, and provide stability over time.

Hack*:* Review and renew systems, processes, and structures to ensure your organisation continues to thrive without your direct involvement.

Exercise*:* Create a detailed succession plan, including identifying potential leaders within your team and defining the processes to ensure business continuity.

Anecdote: A company I worked for implements a great succession planning model at its C-Suite, ensuring that leadership is smoothly transitioned when a senior executive steps down. This foresight helped the company continue growing seamlessly.

Your Example: What steps can you take today to create a plan for organisational continuity in your absence?

47. SHARE YOUR VISION

A common understanding and alignment among a group or organisation regarding long-term goals, values, and desired outcomes unites individuals toward a collective purpose, inspiring collaboration and guiding decisions and actions.

Hack: Clearly articulate your long-term goals to inspire and align your team with a common purpose, creating a shared direction.

Exercise: Host a meeting where you outline your vision for the team's future. Ask for feedback and encourage open dialogue to ensure alignment and commitment.

Your Example: How can you communicate your vision in a way that inspires your team and motivates them to take action?

48. WRITE YOUR LEADERSHIP PHILOSOPHY

A set of personal beliefs, values, and principles that guide how a leader interacts with their team, makes decisions and drives the organisation forward. It is a foundation for their leadership style and influences their actions and decisions.

Hack: Communicate your personal leadership philosophy that reflects your values, principles, and approach to leading others.

Exercise: Write down your leadership philosophy, focusing on how you want to lead and the core values that guide your decisions. Please share it with your team and reflect on it regularly.

Anecdote*:* A CEO shared their leadership philosophy with the organisation, emphasising integrity, collaboration, and continuous improvement. This transparency creates trust and a unified culture.

Your Example*:* What fundamental values define your leadership style, and how do they guide your decision-making?

49. REFLECT ON YOUR LEGACY

Assessing the lasting impact of your leadership on people and the organisation, ensuring your actions align with the positive, enduring influence you want to leave behind.

Hack*:* Regularly evaluate your impact on others and your organisation, adjusting your approach to ensure you leave a meaningful, positive legacy.

Exercise: At the end of each quarter, assess your progress toward your goals and influence on your team and organisation. Use this reflection to adjust your leadership approach.

Your Example: What kind of legacy do you want to leave, and what actions can you take today to move closer to that vision?

50. CHAMPION LIFELONG LEARNING

Continuously pursuing knowledge, skills, and personal growth throughout life to remain adaptable, innovative, and prepared for evolving challenges. Lifelong learning fosters resilience, curiosity, and leadership excellence.

Hack: Stay curious and encourage yourself and your team to embrace learning. Set an example by pursuing professional development opportunities and sharing your insights.

Exercise:

1. Identify one skill or area of knowledge you'd like to improve. Commit to learning something new every quarter through courses, books, or mentorship.
2. Encourage your team to share one learning goal during meetings and discuss how the organisation can support it.

Anecdote: I am constantly learning through attending courses and webinars, reading books and articles and learning from people who share their experiences and knowledge. A leader needs to remain current.

Your Example: How do you prioritise learning in your leadership journey? What steps can you take to cultivate a culture of lifelong learning in your team or organisation?

CONCLUSION

INCLUSIVE LEADERSHIP AS A LIFELONG JOURNEY

Inclusive leadership is not merely a skill but a continuous and transformative journey of growth, learning, and service to others. Throughout this book, I have shared 50 practical leadership hacks, real-world anecdotes, and exercises designed to help you cultivate a leadership style grounded in empathy, equity, and inclusion. Each hack represents a critical building block for creating environments where everyone feels valued, heard, and empowered to contribute their best.

Inclusive leadership requires more than technical expertise or authority; it calls for a mindset of curiosity, humility, and adaptability. It challenges us to look beyond our perspectives, seek out diverse voices, and embrace differences as opportunities for learning and innovation. It demands self-awareness to confront our biases, courage to challenge inequities and a steadfast commitment to fostering belonging for every individual we lead.

CONCLUSION

As you reflect on the insights shared in these pages and integrate them into your leadership practice, remember that inclusive leadership is a dynamic, ongoing process. It evolves with every interaction, every challenge, and every moment of introspection. It is not about being perfect but about being present, intentional, and open to continuous improvement.

The ripple effect of inclusive leadership is profound. When you lead inclusively, you empower individuals and inspire teams to reach their highest potential. You cultivate cultures where diversity is celebrated, equity is embedded, and collaboration thrives. By prioritising inclusivity, you create the conditions for innovation, trust, and long-term success for your organisation and its people.

This book is not the culmination of your leadership journey but a companion for the road ahead. Use it to challenge yourself, deepen your understanding, and take actionable steps toward fostering inclusivity in your leadership approach. Reflect on how these principles apply to your unique context, and always be willing to adapt, learn, and grow. As you close these pages, ask yourself:

- What kind of inclusive leader do you aspire to be?
- How can you create spaces where everyone feels seen and valued? • What legacy of equity and belonging do you want to leave behind?

Inclusive leadership is more than a responsibility; it is an honour and a profound opportunity to impact lives positively. Embrace it with purpose, authenticity, and determination. The world needs leaders who understand the importance of inclusion and live it in every decision they make. Your journey as an inclusive leader continues. Lead boldly and wisely and commit to building a more inclusive world.

Thank you for taking this journey with me. Now, go out and lead with inclusion, empathy, and impact.

RESOURCES

Thomas A. Edison: "I have not failed. I've just found 10,000 ways that won't work." The Socratic Method. (2023, September 27). The Socratic Method. https://www.socratic-method.com/quote-meanings/thoma s-a-edison-i-have-not-failed-ive-just-found-10000-ways-that-wontwork?utm_-source=chatgpt.com

Ranas, C. (2023, March 11). Procrastination and Motivation: A Guide to Overcoming Delay. *Carol Ranas*. https://carolranas.com/uncategor ized/procrastination-and-motivation-a-guide-to-overcoming-delay/

Clarke, T. (2023, February 22). *10 powerful coaching questions to improve your leadership style*. Upskill. https://upskill.consulting/10-powerfulcoaching-questions-to-improve-your-leadership-style/

Kinney, J. (2024, January 15). Maximizing Your Time: 15 Time Management Hacks for Busy entrepreneurs ~ The Busy Llama. *The Busy Llama*. https://www.thebusyllama.com/time-time-managementhacks/

Printed in Great Britain
by Amazon